# HAL•LEONARD
## INSTRUMENTAL PLAY-ALONG

**ONLINE MEDIA INCLUDED**
Audio Recordings
Printable Piano Accompaniments

Speed • Pitch • Balance • Loop

# Classical Solos
## FOR TUBA

### 15 Easy Solos for Contest and Performance

### Arranged by Philip Sparke

To access recordings and PDF accompaniments visit:
**www.halleonard.com/mylibrary**

Enter Code
4964-4097-4886-0120

ISBN 978-1-61780-705-3

**HAL•LEONARD®**
CORPORATION
7777 W. BLUEMOUND RD. P.O. BOX 13819 MILWAUKEE, WI 53213

# WALTZ

**MORITZ VOGEL**
Arranged by PHILIP SPARKE

TUBA

Allegro (♩ = 120)

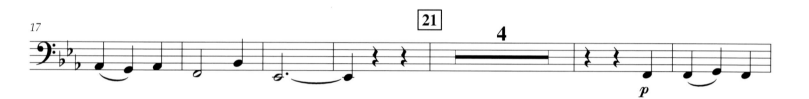

00842553

# CHORALE

## Now praise, my soul, the Lord

TUBA

**JOHANN SEBASTIAN BACH**
Arranged by PHILIP SPARKE

# HUMMING SONG

### from *Album for the Young*

**TUBA**

**ROBERT SCHUMANN**
Arranged by PHILIP SPARKE

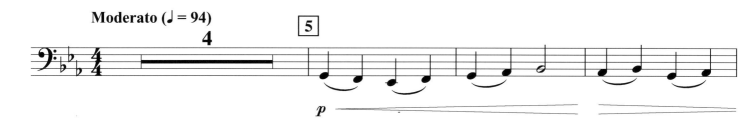

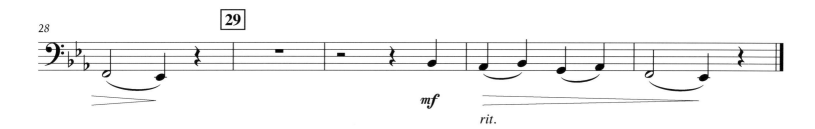

# GYMNOPÉDIE NO. 1

**ERIK SATIE**
Arranged by PHILIP SPARKE

Tuba

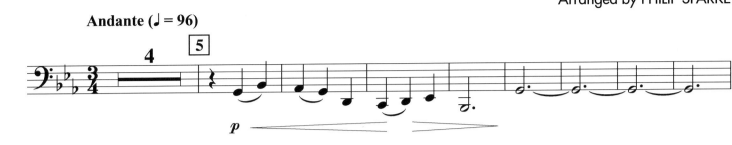

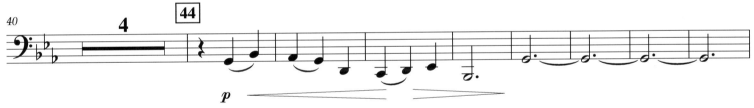

00842553

# I'M CALLED LITTLE BUTTERCUP

### from *HMS Pinafore*

TUBA

**SIR ARTHUR SULLIVAN**
Arranged by PHILIP SPARKE

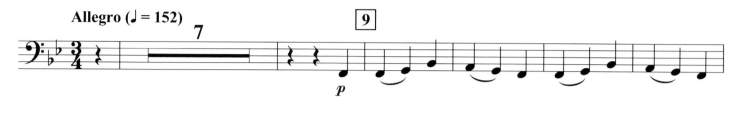

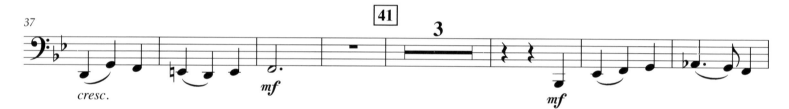

# STUDY

## Op. 37, No. 3

TUBA

HENRY LEMOINE
Arranged by PHILIP SPARKE

00842553

# MINUET

## (Z. 649)

HENRY PURCELL
Arranged by PHILIP SPARKE

TUBA

# THEME AND VARIATION

### from *Sonatina No. 3*

TUBA

**THOMAS ATTWOOD**
Arranged by PHILIP SPARKE

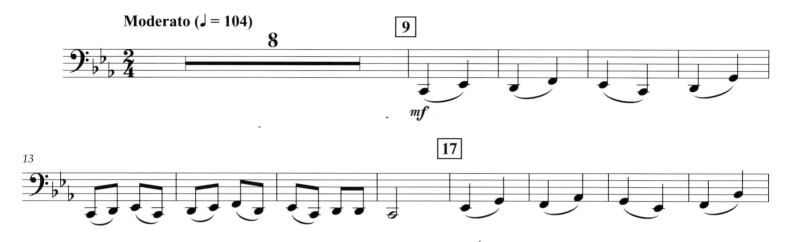

00842553

# NORTHERN SONG

### from *Album for the Young*

**TUBA**

**ROBERT SCHUMANN**
Arranged by PHILIP SPARKE

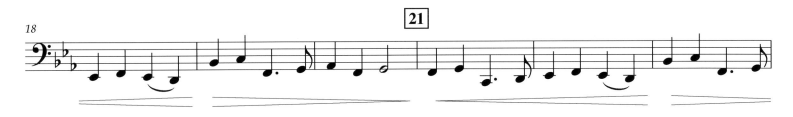

00842553

# TWO GERMAN DANCES

### from *Twelve German Dances, D. 420*

**FRANZ SCHUBERT**
Arranged by PHILIP SPARKE

TUBA

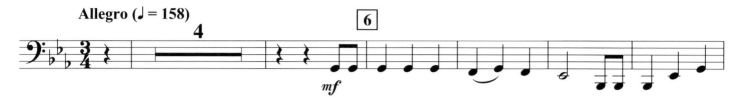

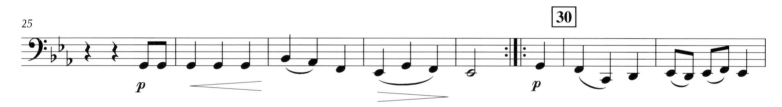

# WATCHMAN'S SONG

### from *Lyric Pieces, Op. 12*

TUBA

**EDVARD GRIEG**
Arranged by PHILIP SPARKE

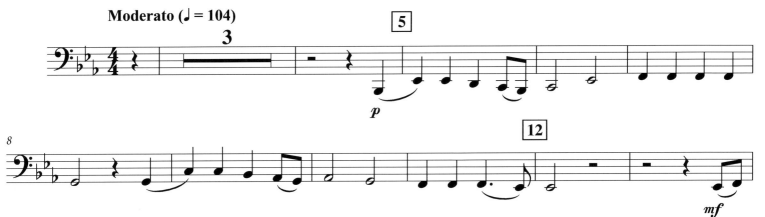

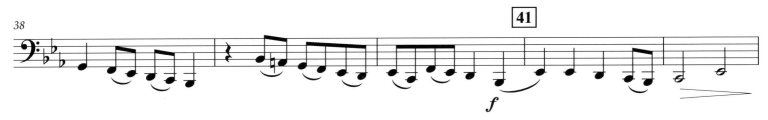

# GAVOTTE

TUBA

JAN LADISLAV DUSSEK
Arranged by PHILIP SPARKE

00842553

# VIEN QUÀ, DORINA BELLA

TUBA

ANTONIO BIANCHI
Transcribed by **C. M. von WEBER**
Arranged by PHILIP SPARKE

Moderato (♩ = 96)

00842553

# MINUET

**from *Notebook for Anna Magdalena Bach***

TUBA

Attributed to **CHRISTIAN PETZOLD**
Arranged by PHILIP SPARKE

*rit.*

00842553

# THE PRINCE OF DENMARK'S MARCH

### from *Choice Lessons for the Harpsichord or Spinet*

TUBA

**JEREMIAH CLARKE**
Arranged by PHILIP SPARKE

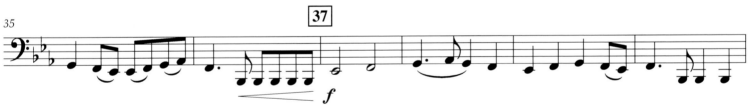